FREE RUNNER

Poems in the Wind

Book 1

By

Karima J. "K2" Sphere
kjsfilms@gmail.com

A Karima C. Johnson Entertainment, First Edition

Copyright © 2014 by Karima J. Sphere

Library of Congress Cataloging-in-Publication Data

Sphere, Karima J.

[Poems, Selection]

Free Runner: Poems in the Wind

ISBN 978-0-692-31214-8 (Paperback)

ISBN 10: 0692312145

Book design by Karima J. Sphere

Manufactured in the United States of America
10 9 8 7 6 5 4 3 2 1

CONTENTS

Acknowledgement

FREE RUNNER: Poems in the Wind (book 1) is a collection of poems based on my life and the snapshots of interesting events I have witnessed. I am grateful for my friends and colleagues who have encouraged me directly and indirectly to start this work, persevere, and publish it.

First and foremost, I want to thank GOD and His Will for allowing me the words to express my thoughts and feelings and the opportunity to capture them on paper.

I would like to acknowledge with gratitude, the love and support of my family and friends - Jeanette Jones, Charles E. Jones, Al-tron L. Jones, Kiisha Arnett, Romelle Johnson, Neal Brown, Sr., Bertha Kenlaw, Cicely France, and Dana McGuire.

I am grateful to the professors and friends at St. Mary's College of Maryland, especially Poet Laureate/Professor Lucille Clifton, Professor Kurt Raney, Professor Michael Glasier, Kam Williams, Ricky Stewart, and The Raw Student Union.

I want to thank my Baltimore poetry family, "Thee Family" who shared their love of the spoken word poetry artform with me - Chuck Maddox and his Black Book of Thoughts, Femi the Dri Fish, Big Man Gary Logan, Romelle - The Mad Poet, and Native Son.

I would like to express appreciation for my Los Angeles-based support team and the organizations dear to my heart - Adrienne Taylor (poetry editor),

Alicia Williams (copy editor), Pernell Marsh, Adrian Zeigler, Organization of Black Screenwriters (OBS), and my fraternity Phi Beta Sigma Fraternity, Inc.

Finally, I thank my love of cinema. It has kept me driven to create beautifully authentic and expressive forms of art.

All proceeds from *Freerunner* will help fund future projects.

I hope you enjoy this book.

The Notorious B.I.G. said it best: *Either you're slingin' crack rock, or you got a wicked jump shot.* Nobody wants to work for it anymore. There's no honor in taking that after school job at Mickey D's. Honor's in the dollar, kid. So I went the college boy way of slinging crack rock. I became a stockbroker. But, in my case, I became a filmmaker.

--Karima J. Sphere
(Inspired by the movie *Boiler Room*)

FREE RUNNER

In 2013, I became a free runner

'Cause I heard on the news

The Panda Bear will be extinct a generation from now,

And nobody gives a funk about the Polar Bear

Nobody effed with the Grizzly Bear,

No one gave no never mind about the Black Bear.

And I stand here bare-chested in my speech

Trying to reach a higher understanding in all of this

At the age of 33, my own place, my own ride, my own drive,

With good health, good lovin', good job, and no kids.

I am no longer the predator.

I am the prey.

'Cause sistahs are looking for emotionally-available brothers,

And I pray I end up with a good one.

Flipside or same side

Depending on your realities--clear side.

There are some California Follies

With the sweetest venom,

The kindest smile,

The gentlest touch

With those innocent eyes.

Oh, so innocent eyes...

Hoodies came in handy

As she tried to candy-yam me, up

When she found out, I was a good one.

Inside or Southside--along side

For the true queens out there,

With a scent like yours,

You had to be the softer side of Sears.

Better yet, the softest side of tears.

She asked me, "How you want me baby?"

"Girl, I want you backwards in reversible slacks."

Better yet, I want your crouching tiger in crotchless panties

And you don't know the severity of how I be trying to get at you.

Eastside or Westside--real side

It became diabolical for a free runner

'Cause God didn't give me any powers to be a super villain

And a villain I would be.

Like the way the world saw Jesus

Lost in translation.

Like the way the world sees Jesús

Misunderstood in his movements.

Saying, "He crossed the border,"

When the border crossed him.

Outside or Pharcyde

Depending on your realities—darkside,

I have been here for nine years,

And I've known three people who killed themselves.

So, I damn sure wasn't suicidal, but I was ready to go.

Ready to skyscrape off this building

Launching my body through the air and land where I can.

'Cause living was difficult to say the least

Especially when life comes at you in factions.

Had to be surgical

Divide myself into fractions

Fifty-one-fifty in my head.

Thirty-three percent of my imagination stashed under my bed.

Seventeen percent hurled through the world with pinpoint accuracy

to this place here.

And I swear to you I will live free,

Or *Die Hard* in this Hollywood-land.

Rockside or Hardside--downside

The wind imported too many lost angels

Trying to escape the crates of their *Bourne Identity*

And I wish to God they knew it

Like I know old school Tonka toys

'Cause it will certainly bust you up before you bust it up.

I hope you hear me.

Knowing, I'm not another Rob Stapleton talking about eight dollars.

I'm talking about free running.

A LOVE SUPREME

A Love Supreme, A Love Supreme
A Love Supreme, A Love Supreme

I mean
You are my queen
Dreams couldn't hold water
Nor my attention
Like you did
When you smiled at me.
We, I believed to be some chain reaction
From the heavens
Sent here by the clouds
To show sunrays how to act.
In fact,
Plants are envious of our proximity
Because we, baby, are closer than
Their own asexual reproduction
Eruption from our center
Where we enter into perfect union.

A Love Supreme
A Love Supreme
A Love Supreme

It will be a time
When all this arguing will
Feel stupid and trivial
And the most honest thing
To say is...
I've missed you.
'Cause love is too expensive

To be joked or played with
So I insist in making you smile
'Cause you make me smile.
And could you,
Would you please?
Stay for a while.

> *A Love Supreme*
> *A Love Supreme*
> *A Love Supreme*

I want to learn how to
Hand dance with you.
I believe she is here.
She, the woman, who makes my heart
Dance like glitter falling
From a New York New Year's celebration
She is here now.
Seemingly, far past my outstretched hands,
She enters the room.
Moments after I leave
Getting off the bus.
As I get on the bus,
And in my travels,
As I keep my fingers crossed,
Awaiting, patiently the hand of chance
That will include me with you.

> *A Love Supreme*
> *A Love Supreme*
> *A Love Supreme*

When we finally meet
Like anything real and lasting,
It will be times when
You or I or both
Will prefer in a breath
Loneliness over stress.
That will be our test.
Will we have something relentless and true?
As everyone else before us,
Will have only spoken
A premise, a riddle, a joke,
Or a clue.

A Love Supreme
A Love Supreme
A Love Sur-pre-eme

"I hate to see you go,
but I love to watch you walk away."

ICON: REVISING IN THE DARK
For Poet Laureate Lucille Clifton

Midnight over me
Car lights in face
Yet you claim to not see me
Needing me for your money
And your quota.
Incense smoke surrounds my personal space
And nobody knows my sadness.

Emergency!!!
Somebody call the cops on this crazy fool!
On this crazy fad
On this crazy color
Everybody trying to be like me
like black is a seasonal color.
We are people
Not t-shirts.
Icon stopped for no damn reason
But he must have done something
Deviant
Labeled deviant at birth
Look at me
Really, look at me.
Know me
Change.
Even Arthur Ashe was black-listed
Bad ass black male
Bad intentions presumed.
See me as I am.

14

Taken from my land,
Taken from my momma's hand,
Blown away from knowing me.

Incense ease my pain.
I see signs.
Failure they say.
I will fail.
Forget them who say I will fail.
Icon. . . yield, black man.
No rights during school hours
This world with its color code
Too black
Not black enough
Too much melanin
Downgrading me,
Yet you want to sell my shadow.
Prices pasted on my forehead.
It's hip to talk black,
Walk black,
Jive black,
Wear black,
With a little white collar in America.
White collars make us look successful.
Is it the way we lean in our Lexuses that says,
"we're doing okay?"

When you think of me,
Think Ebony golden chocolate almond-dipped
beautiful.
That's not like I had to write it down to know it.
I am an icon of my color.

WANTING TO BE LOVED HAS GOT ME TRIPPIN'

In the middle of saying little
and saying nothing,
I say too much.

I wave hi.
I say, "hi."
I mean *hiiii.*
I ask you how your day was
to break into conversation with you.
If she is not, Her,
I wish it to be Her on the sun-dipped lips.
I wish to kiss and suck,
and a kiss is maybe the only promising thing
to ask for.

See, man,
I was convinced that money was the way to go
because I ain't never,
I ain't ever,
"DENZEL, Denzel!!!"
I ain't never see women excited,
Especially over an average positive-thinking Joe.
And so, in the middle of a fire,
I heard someone speak...

> *Throw down your wallet,**
> *Throw down your wallet,*
> *We all don't have to suffer.*

Who's that?
> Don't ask.

What's that?
> Don't ask.

When did you?
> Don't ask.

Why did you?
> Don't ask.

How did you?
> Don't ask.

Yet, I would like to know you anyway,
'cause my only secret wish was for us
to be a double vowel.
You the first
and me the second.
Silently listening
to your heart beating,
Waiting for sentences to merge,
With my ear drums again
and again.
Maybe you'll spend the night
With my thoughts again...
First there was fuckin',
Then commitment,
Then there was that fucking commitment.

In the shores off the coast of Jersey barriers,
I found love on a two-way street.
And before I knew it again,
I lost myself on a one-lane highway.
Fellows know

curves are sometimes too sharp to keep your focus
when eyes meet and greet.
With long-lash kisses
no time to pause…to re-enlist
"Is this real?"
As cheeks are red flares bursting
in the honeysuckle silence of Spring air,
"Wanting to be loved has got me, trippin'."

WHITE ZINFANDEL

When I fall in love, it will be forever.

I've missed being called "baby"
by any woman.
Missed the scent of a woman,
left on my hand
brushing against her cheek,
missed holding waists, synchronizing
movements with a kiss.
Missed finding the prettiest spot in my memory
and sharing it with you.
Missed those sexy looks at me.
Missed feeding you fruit,
naked.

I've missed speaking
in an unspoken language
handing you a cool drink before
asking for it.
Anticipating, sipping
White Zinfandel inside your essence
sucking on your bottom lip.
Touching you with my tongue
running down the sweat of your back
licking moisture from curves
slurring words that come
in between induced moans.
Missed palms clenching
soft knuckles
legs gripping sides of thighs.
teeth biting bed sheets
toes intertwining
with love
missed making your leg jump!

I've missed being called "baby"
by any woman.
Missed smiles that make me
want to stay longer.
Missed a sunset someone
to take my time with to please.
Setting your mind at ease
in a shower with me.
Missed kisses complimenting tattoos.
And I can't deny
I've wanted you since
our words touched each other.

On a hot summer evening, I could eat a peach for
days.

SWEET LOVE 1

Sweet Love,

after the coincidences

If this be true,

What I feel for you

Is I do love you

and time will shower me wonderfully true

in thine eyes, sweet love's fire.

For you have sparked coals in phoenix wings

that blaze October skies

With depth and enchanted wishes

I long to hold time in place to listless days

that dance in delicate cadence in song for you,

Sweet Love.

BRAZENFACED

If there was no God…
I would have killed you with these words before I
spoke.
I would have pissed in corners of pages
and called it art.
I would have pulled out my weapon,
Defaming negros with my size
And asshole would be my pen name.

If there was no God…
I would pace to keep pace with this Charmed City
"That bitch's place"
would be my favorite eating establishment
And they would stop tugging on me,
'Cause M&Ms make me shit.

If there was no God…
I would look at you sideways
with a brick in the other hand,
Looking at you crazy
like Richard Pryor in *Stir Crazy*.
And _____.com would be my email address.
You would always find me sleeping.
There would be no freeways,
just more highways
And higher ways of living inside this L.A. Rubik's
Cube.

If there were no God…
Anger would be more than my sister's mother's

Brother's niece's uncle--twice removed.
It would be all of our fathers,
and we would all love to experience incest.
My consciousness on the mic would be all the rush I
needed,
And "peace out man" would be one finger.

If there was no God...
The rat race would begin today
with my foot on somebody's neck.
Love would be some flash card
that reminded me of my Jeep.
Kanye West's *Black Skinhead*
would be my theme song
instead of any version of *California Dreaming.*

If there were no God...
My face would shadow the blue shade of midnight oil
paintings.
Eyes-Stare-Dead-Tight-Angle-Straight-To-Hell
I would tell you
I'm death in dreams.
You would believe me,
and I would rip apart
the rainbow connection
between the lovers,
the dreamers,
and me.

A DIRTY PENNY

I approached
only after careful consideration
about how I feel about you.
Seriously caught up.
Renting room in my head for you.
Hoping you would understand that I wasn't playing
And as I spilled my song and dance.
I had my fingers crossed
Hoping you would look into my heart
and this was a loving chance between
ONE + ONE = TWO
into ONE wonderful existence.
Wishing you would be my queen,
and I would be your king until time ended,
but this, THIS HERE, is too much like right.
Time passes and I don't reminisce off of spite.
Your response to my sincere honesty blew a fuse,
left me confused, inside in the dark.
I thought this is what you wanted
Straight-up and blunt.
Without being blunted.
Your response was like
I was at a job interview.

THAT-YOU-I-MEAN-I-KIND-OF-
SORT-OF-DIDN'T-MAYBE
-DIDN'T-FIT-THE-PROFILE-
YET-LOVE-WAS-IN-THE-AIR-
FAR-FROM-HERE-
AND-THAT-WAS-A-CUTE-RESPONSE

Just left me thirsty for some passion fruit
shared between two souls
that would obliterate the obstacles
because I wanted to build up fortresses of love
between us on the plains of reality.
Professing us boldly
so all the world would see our lovemaking--
Our mental, spiritual, physical,
Sexual awakening.
Retaining something real.
Now here comes today
What I've come here to say is...
I didn't open my mouth for the thrill of stealing your
heart
or to get sacked like I did.
But since you see me as just
"a dirty penny"
and not one of the last of its kind,
valuable buffalo nickels
I refuse to,
continue to,
want to,
chase
you.

Hmm.
As I thumb through your CD collection
for the last time
checking out the selection
finding only one jazz CD playing.
Beside my soul's and spirit's reflection
I see, "You must love R&B."
Playing Your Game, Baby

Your game, Baby
Playing Your Game, Baby
Your game, Baby...

WHERE LOVE MEANS NOTHING

If you stand outside long enough in the winter time,
the cold breeze doesn't bother you.

In my sleep,
I linger for a while
in my 5 to 6 hours of rest.
Resting from the daily test.
Then, before I know it,
again, I am slammed forward
like the end of a roller coaster ride.
No longer can I be shy
as I am cast out into the streets like old pennies
when hoodlums break into antique vending machines.
And there are many games
where love means nothing.
You can't have a long-term somethin' for nothin'
and quickly I got tired of playing those games.
Maybe I need to leave this place.
Maybe I need to conquer my own space.
Maybe I've been hurt too many times
in my center of centers
where light bends back into the darkness
behind the dual moons
that hides my truest of true smiles.

As I stare at the palms of my hands,
I try to hold back the forming of fists
to shake at the winters of my discontent.
I was bent from the time of day
because it was told to me
that you can't have your pride and mo'ney.
Choose one and bruise the other.
It had nothing to do with color.
It was about living life as best you saw it.
Every dollar that circulates

has a *little* cocaine on it.
In the changing of hands, it stands for division.
Those that have it
and those that want it
seem to be all blunted by the mighty dollar.

Money made the world go around,
and money made the world go around,
Money made the world go around.

We waited for God to step in
and show us the way.
Seen as a runaway with high hopes,
I couldn't keep pace with the high rollers.
So she hung me loose from her bra strap
saying, "When he blows up,
I'll be close enough to catch the discharge."
Yet, mentally I was large.
All in time, I said to myself.
All in time.
So, I had to dismiss her.
I didn't want to get caught
licking my lips longing for too much candy.

AS YOU REFRESHEN YOUR DRINK
Dedicated to Ricky Stewart

Weed
could only keep me diluted and assimilated.
Too massive to be locked down
and I just found out now that the worst thing in life
is not death.
It is screaming out your name
and not being heard.
"What's the word?!"
"Freedom for your momma!
Freedom for your sister!
Freedom for your brother!
but no freedom for me."

As the search continues,
shorties holler out,
"Who got game?"
Only pursuing those that gleam green. . .
She said, "She was looking for money."
So I told her, "I was looking for ass."
Trying to sound crass,
I thought a better quest, question would be,
"Who got God?"
Life was hard, almost didn't make it to the door
"Momma, I'm not happy here."
"Momma, I want to go home."
"Which way is home?"
I know it's somewhere away,
not here,
not now,
but for right now,

I'm in need of help to hold on.
At minimum, a hug to hold on,
and I've lost so much
that they see me as heartless
wanting to depart from this.
At times, words come out artless on the River Styx
because the surface tension can turn chaotic.
In the second coming of the storms,
I hope to reform,
transform into a Hi-Lite
into a blue light form.

As you refreshen your drink,
I hope to speak some truth
and not no hustle--
truth and not some hustle.
The real revolution is the fight within,
but to me, my soldiers seem to be marching too slowly.
Lowly is my compassion when dealing with people of
this world.
So I apologize to me, my God, and you
because sometimes god-brothers act like the foolish
when they take kindness for a weakness.
Sweetness would be
if the Million Man March was every day;
the queen for me was beside me;
and, I wasn't labeled as a Black Haitian
because I ain't from here.
Too near the drowning well to hear you call for more
confusion,
as many only trust only lust
because it was
"Giving you something you could feel."

And as you refreshen your drink,
I had to get busy living
or get busy dying.

As I bled to death, as my very life oozed out of me, all I could think of was something the great Negro James Baldwin had written. "People pay for what they do, and still more of what they have allowed themselves to become, and they pay for it, very simply, by the lives they lead.

--Pierre Delacroix
(from the movie *Bamboozled*)

Glossary of Terms

FREE RUNNER

- **Free Runner-** is individual who practices the art of expressing oneself in his or her environment without limitation of movement
- **No never mind-** denoting something far less likely
- **Follies-** women who appear to be quality, but who are full of calamity and foolery
- **Hoodies-** is another name for condoms
- **Crouching tiger** – is another name for female genitalia
- **Pharcyde-** a dark place inside yourself where you are alone with your thoughts
- **Skyscrape** –to leap from a high place
- **Fifty-one-fifty** -Is a person suspected of having mental disorder that makes them a danger to self, a danger to others, and/or gravely disabled in the California Welfare and Institutions Code.
- **Hollywood-land-** The original name for Hollywood
- *Bourne Identity- Chained to the past while in search for ones true self*
- *Rob Stapleton-* is an actor, writer, comedian known for <u>Mike Epps Presents: Live from Club Nokia</u>

A LOVE SUPREME

- **Love Supreme-** *The mantra of John Coltrane's song "Love Supreme"*

ICON: REVISING IN THE DARK

- **Arthur Ashe-** Iconic African-American Tennis star

WANTING TO BE LOVED HAS GOT ME TRIPPIN'

- **Her-** The woman of my dreams
- **Denzel-** refers to Denzel Washington
- **Throw down your wallet-** (from Martin Lawrence, You so Crazy)
- **Jersey barriers-** is a modular concrete or plastic barrier employed to separate lanes of traffic. Also known as a K-rail

BRAZENFACED

- **Charmed City-** nickname for Baltimore City, Maryland
- **Blank SPACE-** a noted space allowing for variation in the performance of poem
- **Rainbow Connection-** "The Rainbow Connection" was written for The Muppet Movie and was nominated for an Academy Award for Best Song in 1979. It is sung by Kermit as the movie's opening number

A DIRTY PENNY —(Appears in Men Heartbreak Anthology —pg7)

- **Blunt-** saying or expressing something in a very direct way
- **Blunted-** being under the influence of marijuana
- **Playing your game baby-** The chorus of Barry White's song "Playing Your Game Baby"

AS YOU REFRESHEN YOUR DRINK

- **River Styx-** is a river in Greek mythology that formed the boundary between Earth and the Underworld

Karima J. "K2" Sphere, born Karima Chew Johnson, October 18, 1974, is a Poet, Screenwriter, Playwright, and Filmmaker whose artistic works reflect his unique and authentic take on life.

Sphere was born in Baltimore City, Maryland where he received his diploma from the third oldest public high school in the nation - Baltimore City College.

After graduating, he continued on to St. Mary's College of Maryland, Public Honors College. It is one of only two institutions with this designation in the United States.

During his time at St. Mary's College, Sphere began searching for ways to incorporate all elements of his artistic talent into each of his projects.

As an event coordinator at St. Mary's, he wrote, directed, and produced a series of commercials promoting spoken word. It was his unique expression of this burgeoning form of art that helped foster a relationship between the college and the spoken word poets of Washington D.C., Maryland, and Virginia (DMV).

In 1998, after graduating with a degree in Political Science, Karima Sphere returned to his roots in Baltimore to help his family and fulfill a lifelong goal of giving back to his community.

While in Baltimore, Sphere became the first African-American Intern for the Ad Council and worked on the Welfare-to-Work Program. It was during this time, that he also helped form a spoken word poetry group titled "Thee Family."

The newly formed group became well-known in the Baltimore area, amassing a large poetry following. Many even considered Thee Family reminiscent of the Last Poets. They toured the region, authored books, and even produced CDs.

In 1999, Sphere began teaching fourth grade at Edgecombe Middle School. Soon after, he had a dream that would alter his life path. Immediately, he moved to Los Angeles in 2004 and became a member of OBS (Organization of Black Screenwriters).

By 2005, Sphere had written, directed, and produced his first short film, "Finding the Boom-Bap" - a metaphor for finding love through a perfect blend of Beat and Melody. The film premiered at Oberhausen International Film Festival.

In 2010, Sphere wrote and produced the Documentary Web Series, "Web Series - Hollywood Stories" - an illuminating documentary about the lives and challenges of people living their dreams in Hollywood. The series garned over 42,000 downloads worldwide.

He became lead writer and a co-producer for the 2014 short suspense film,"The Ultimate Prize", which premiered at the 48-Hour Film Festival. Sphere also authored his first book, _Freerunner_ - an infusion of poetic art involving spoken word and free verse poetry.

Currently, Sphere is in pre-production for his horror feature, "Auction Day: Grudge Fire Chronicles," working on his second poetry book, "The Rebuttal Book," and co-writing his first play, "The Poindexters."

www.ingramcontent.com/pod-product-compliance
Lightning Source LLC
Chambersburg PA
CBHW060646030426

42337CB00018B/3466